LESSONS ON LIVING FROM
JEREMIAH

A devotional by
WOODROW KROLL

BACK TO THE BIBLE
Publishing

JEREMIAH
published by Back to the Bible Publishing
©1998 by Woodrow Kroll

International Standard Book Number
0-8474-0689-X

Edited by Rachel Derowitsch
Cover design by Robert Greuter
& Associates

For information:
BACK TO THE BIBLE
POST OFFICE BOX 82808
LINCOLN, NEBRASKA 68501

1 2 3 4 5 6 7 8—04 03 02 01 00 99 98

Printed in the USA

CONTENTS

DAY 1

Jeremiah 1:4-5

Then the word of the LORD came to me, saying: "Before I formed you in the womb I knew you; before you were born I sanctified you; and I ordained you a prophet to the nations."

Known by God

Those who know their geography well might know that the longest place name still in use is Taumatawhakatangi-hangakoauauotamateaturipukakapiki-maungahoronukupokaiwenuakitanatahu, a New Zealand hill. Or they might be aware that the full name of Los Angeles is El Pueblo de Nuestra Senora la Reina de los Angeles de Porciuncula, which can be abbreviated to 3.63 percent of its size by simply calling it L.A. But no one can know a subject as well as God knows us.

When God revealed Himself to Jeremiah, it was with the assurance that He was acquainted with this Old Testament prophet more intimately than anyone else ever could be. God knew Jeremiah before he was formed in his mother's womb. Even before he was born, God had set him aside to fulfill the role of a prophet to the nations. He knew Jeremiah as a person and He knew what He had in store for him. In fact, there was nothing about Jeremiah and his situation that God didn't know.

We also can believe with assurance that there is nothing about us or our lives that is beyond the knowledge of God. He even knows the exact number of hairs on our heads (Matt. 10:30). He has mapped out a blueprint for our lives that may hold surprises for us, but not for Him. Like a master craftsman, He is shaping and molding us to fit His plans.

You need not be fearful about your future. God knows you intimately. He knows exactly the things to bring into your life and leave out of your life that will prepare *you* for the things He has prepared for *you*.

The God who knows you best knows the best for you.

Reflections/Prayer Requests

_____

_____

_____

_____

_____

_____

_____

_____

DAY 2

Jeremiah 3:4

*"Will you not from this time cry to Me, 'My fa-
ther, You are the guide of my youth?'"*

A Guide From Our Youth

The life of Edgar Allen Poe is one of the most tragic of all American writers. Raised by foster parents who loved him deeply, he was provided with an education that matched his genius. But then Poe lost his young bride through tuberculosis. By that time alcohol and drug abuse, along with involvement in the occult and Satanism, worked to destroy him. Depression and insanity plagued his short life, eventually leaving him unconscious in the gutter of a street in Baltimore. Four days later he died, never regaining consciousness. Poe began his life with money and brilliance, but in his latter years he became a ragged, penniless bum.

Israel also started well. As a young nation, the Jews looked to God for guidance. But as the years passed and God blessed her with prosperity, she strayed from His instructions. Israel prostituted herself with other gods (Jer. 3:2) and forgot her original commitment to the Lord. As a result, drought came upon the land—not simply as a punishment, but as God's way to get Israel to return to the guide of her youth.

Only as she followed the One who had guided her in her younger years could Israel hope to be successful as a nation.

Too often those who grow up in the church, who attend Sunday school and youth group, who sit under the preaching of God's Word, forget the One who guided them in their youth. As they move out into the world, they often move away from the Lord, who led them through the difficult years of growing up. The consequences are frequently devastating.

If you have left the Guide of your youth, return to Him today. He waits for you. Call out to Him as your Heavenly Father and recommit yourself to His guidance. Let His showers of blessings end the drought in your life.

Let the Guide of your youth be the Guide of your life.

Reflections/Prayer Requests

_____

_____

_____

_____

_____

_____

_____

_____

DAY 3

Jeremiah 5:31

The prophets prophesy falsely, and the priests rule by their own power; and My people love to have it so. But what will you do in the end?

In the End

Everything that begins also ends. Beautiful buildings are erected, but eventually they are torn down. Seeds sprout and grow into plants, but after their season they, too, come to an end. Even the universe, as we now know it, will some day be destroyed (Rev. 21:1). It is only reasonable, then, that as we begin something we must keep in mind that it eventually will come to an end—and then what?

That was God's warning to Israel. They were being misled by those who were responsible for their spiritual welfare. The prophets and priests were telling the people only what they wanted to hear, which was fine with them. They didn't want to be confronted with their sins. They loved the sugarcoated messages and the false assurances. But God inquired, "What will you do in the end?" What will you do when reality knocks on the door and you no longer can continue to deny the truth? Everything that begins has an end—and then what will you do?

8

As you live your life, don't forget that one day it, too, will end. And then what? God's Word indicates that all Christians must stand before the Judgment Seat of Christ to give an account of ourselves (Rom. 14:10; 2 Cor. 5:10). This is not to determine our salvation but the value of our works. All those things that are built upon the lies of the world are only wood, hay and straw, and they will be burned up (1 Cor. 3:12-15). In the end, only what you have done for Christ will last.

As you go through your day, evaluate what you do in light of the end you know is coming. When you stand before the Judgment Seat of Christ, will the things you've given your life to really matter? Commit yourself to do that which is of eternal value.

The end is coming—and then what will you do?

Reflections/Prayer Requests

_____

_____

_____

_____

_____

_____

DAY 4

Jeremiah 6:14

"They have also healed the hurt of My people slightly, saying, 'Peace, Peace!' when there is no peace."

Wishful Thinking

On Wake Island in 1950, President Truman said to Gen. Douglas MacArthur, "I want only three words as my epitaph—'He Brought Peace.'" That was certainly a worthy and noble ambition, yet how elusive and disappointing the hope! Since the days of Truman, the United States has been involved in two major military actions, the Korean War and the Vietnam War, plus numerous smaller skirmishes. The desire for peace has been admirable, but so far it's only been wishful thinking.

The leaders of Israel also had high hopes of peace. The prophets and priests announced that God would keep them safe (Jer. 28:2). Israel would not be pulled into the conflict around them. They would not fall victim to the advancing Babylonian army. Yet it was all wishful thinking. By 605 B.C. Babylon occupied Judah, and in 586 B.C. the armies of Nebuchadnezzar besieged and overthrew Jerusalem (39:1-10). The majority of people were carried into captivity and their hopes for peace, fueled by the false claims of their leaders, turned out to be nothing more than wishful thinking.

God offers a peace that is more than wishful thinking—it's a reality. This is not a peace, however, between opposing armies. Instead, it's a peace treaty between ourselves and Him. When we receive Jesus Christ as our Savior, the hostility between God and us is put to rest. The apostle Paul says, "Therefore, having been justified by faith, we have peace with God through our Lord Jesus Christ" (Rom. 5:1).

If you have that peace with God today, give thanks. No one can take it away from you. No matter what your circumstances are, your peace with Him will never change. If you don't have that peace through Christ, you can receive it by surrendering your life to Jesus and accepting the payment of His shed blood at Calvary to atone for your sins. And that's not just wishful thinking—that's reality!

Don't settle for wishful thinking; make peace in your heart a reality.

Reflections/Prayer Requests

_____

_____

_____

_____

_____

DAY 5

Jeremiah 7:23

"But this is what I commanded them, saying, 'Obey My voice, and I will be your God, and you shall be My people. And walk in all the ways that I have commanded you, that it may be well with you.'"

Obey My Voice

A young son of a missionary couple in Zaire was playing in the yard. Suddenly the voice of the boy's father rang out from the porch, "Philip, obey me instantly! Drop to your stomach!" Immediately the youngster did as his father commanded. "Now crawl toward me as fast as you can!" The boy obeyed. "Stand up and run to me!" Philip responded unquestioningly and ran to his father's arms. As the youngster turned to look at the tree by which he had been playing, he saw a large deadly snake hanging from one of the branches! His father's commands were not issued out of cruelty but for his well-being.

God's commands to the Israelites were given for the same reasons. He wanted the absolute best for them. He assured them through the prophet Jeremiah that His purpose in requiring obedience from them was "that it may be well with you." His heartfelt intent for the people of Israel was that they might enjoy a loving relationship with Him and, at the same time, avoid the sin that was destroying the nations around them.

God wants to control your life also—not for the sake of ruling over you, but because He desires the very best for you. He wants you to enjoy a fulfilling, purposeful and meaningful life with as little distress brought about by sin as possible. His commandments are to make your life more enjoyable, not miserable.

If you feel that your life is being limited by God's commandments, remember their intent. In His infinite wisdom, the Lord knows what will make you happy, not just for today but for all of eternity. Instead of arguing with God or resisting Him, embrace all that He asks, "that it may be well for you."

Obedience is not just good for you; it's best for you.

Reflections/Prayer Requests

_____

_____

_____

_____

_____

_____

_____

DAY 6

Jeremiah 8:5

"Why then has this people slidden back, Jerusalem, in a perpetual backsliding? They hold fast to deceit, they refuse to return."

Backslidden

Robert Robinson was saved out of a tempestuous life of sin. Shortly after that, at the age of 23, Robinson wrote the hymn "Come, Thou Fount." Sometime later, however, he wandered far from the Lord. One day he was traveling by stagecoach and sat beside a young woman engrossed in a book. In God's providence, she ran across a verse she thought was beautiful and asked him what he thought of it. "Prone to wander, Lord, I feel it, prone to leave the God I love." Bursting into tears, Robinson said, "Madam, I am the poor, unhappy man who wrote that hymn many years ago, and I would give a thousand worlds, if I had them, to enjoy the feelings I had then."

The people of ancient Israel knew that situation very well. They, too, were backslidden. In fact, they had reached such a state in their backsliding that they preferred deceit to truth and stubbornly refused to respond to God's plea through Jeremiah to repent. The only option left was judgment. Before Jeremiah's ministry was finished, the city would fall to the Babylonians and the people would be taken into captivity.

There is no one more unhappy than a Christian out of fellowship with His Lord. Not only does this condition bring sorrow to the backslider, but ultimately it brings judgment from God. He loves His children too much to let them continue in this condition without His intervention. He knows they're being robbed of all the good He has designed for them.

If you find yourself today farther away from the Lord than you once were, you've backslidden and you're courting God's judgment. Right now is the time to do something about it. Repent of your sins, confess them and be restored to fellowship with the Lord. If you will judge yourself, God won't have to do it for you.

If you're going in the wrong direction, turning around is the only right direction.

Reflections/Prayer Requests

_____

_____

_____

_____

_____

DAY 7

Jeremiah 8:20

"The harvest is past, the summer is ended, and we are not saved!"

Too Late!

The ancient city of Pompeii is less than a mile from the foot of Mount Vesuvius. In the summer of A.D. 79, Vesuvius erupted suddenly and with great violence. Hot ash, stones and cinders rained down on the city and the air became filled with poisonous gases. Most of the people escaped, but not all. Among the approximately 200 remains that have been found was one of a woman with her jewels in her hands. Apparently she had spent her time gathering her treasures instead of fleeing from the doomed city. Because of her delay, she lost both her jewels and her life.

As Jeremiah contemplated his own people, he came to a similar conclusion. God had sent warning after warning to Israel through various prophets. Even at the eleventh hour, the Lord raised up Jeremiah to call the people to repentance. But they refused to heed him. Their response was to plot against God's prophet (Jer. 18:18) and eventually to throw him into a mud-filled cistern (38:6). As Jeremiah saw it, the people had reached a point of no return. They had squandered their time in fruitless pursuits and, in their delay, they had missed the opportunity to experience God's salvation. The Babylonian army was at their doorstep and judgment was at hand.

God is gracious and gives us many warnings. His desire is always for repentance rather than judgment. But such warnings must be heeded before it's too late. One day—you don't know when—death will close the door to your opportunity to get right with God. Hebrews 9:27 says, "It is appointed for men to die once, but after this the judgment." The Bible is very clear: there are no second chances; there is only judgment.

Listen to God today. Respond to His call without delay. When the time for repentance is past, it's gone forever.

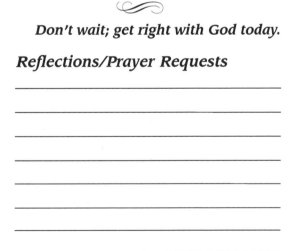

Don't wait; get right with God today.

Reflections/Prayer Requests

_____

_____

_____

_____

_____

_____

_____

_____

DAY 8

Thus says the LORD: "Let not the wise man glory in his wisdom, let not the mighty man glory in his might, nor let the rich man glory in his riches; but let him who glories glory in this, that he understands and knows Me, that I am the LORD, exercising lovingkindness, judgment, and righteousness in the earth. For in these I delight," says the LORD."

How to Find Glory

People find many things to glory in and brag about. For the runner, it might be his speed or distance. For the weight lifter, it's the number of pounds he can curl. For the scholar, it might be his list of degrees or publications. For the wealthy man, it's his diverse portfolio. But none of these things bring a glory that will last forever. They are at best a passing grandeur.

Speaking through the prophet Jeremiah, God exhorted His people not to look for their glory in wisdom, power or wealth but in their relationship with Him. It was not the armies that defended God's holy city, Jerusalem; it was not the silver and gold in the temple treasury. Israel could brag about none of these things. What was really important, what would bring glory forever, was the opportunity to grow in a relationship with the Lord. To understand and know God was something to boast about. That was all that mattered.

People frantically seek for their 15 minutes of fame, their moment in the limelight. They spend vast sums of money and even risk their lives to stake a fleeting claim to glory. Others try to bask in the reflected glory of the rich and famous. But none of these things are truly satisfying, let alone lasting. Only God can offer that.

Find your glory today in your relationship with Christ. Make it the most important part of your life. Seek to grow more intimate each day with your Lord and Savior by daily reading His Word, enjoying His presence and talking with Him in prayer. When you know Him intimately, you have something worth bragging about.

Glory in Christ and you can bask in His light forever.

Reflections/Prayer Requests

_____

_____

_____

_____

_____

_____

_____

_____

DAY 9

Jeremiah 11:13-14

"For according to the number of your cities were your gods, O Judah; and according to the number of the streets of Jerusalem you have set up altars to that shameful thing, altars to burn incense to Baal. Therefore do not pray for this people, or lift up a cry or prayer for them; for I will not hear them in the time that they cry out to Me because of their trouble."

When God Won't Hear

Two men were talking one day. One of them said, "My wife talks to herself a lot." His friend answered, "Mine does too, but she doesn't know it. She thinks I'm listening."

Many Christians are like that. They pray, thinking that they are being heard, but God isn't listening. Likewise, Israel placed a great emphasis on prayer. David said that he prayed every morning (Ps. 5:3; 88:13; 143:8). The sons of Korah exclaimed, "O LORD, God of my salvation, I have cried out day and night before You" (Ps. 88:1). Without question, such devotion is commendable. But the people of Jeremiah's day had so profaned their relationship with the Lord that He said, "I will not hear them in the time that they cry out to Me because of their trouble."

Sin interferes with our prayer life. God cannot honor our requests for help when we need to ask for His forgiveness instead. It's amazing how quickly we turn to prayer when we face problems and expect God to deliver us. Yet we are filled with indifference or even outright defiance the rest of the time. In such situations God says, "I'm not listening."

If you are not seeing answers to your prayers, make sure that there is no known sin in your life that is preventing God from responding (Ps. 66:18). Confess your sin and get rid of those attitudes or actions you know can't be pleasing to God, and then the road will be cleared for Him to answer your requests. Claim the cleansing blood of Christ to open the pipeline of prayer.

Prayer only works when the channels are open.

Reflections/Prayer Requests

_____

_____

_____

_____

_____

_____

_____

DAY 10

Jeremiah 12:1

Righteous are You, O LORD, when I plead with You; yet let me talk with You about Your judgments. Why does the way of the wicked prosper? Why are those happy who deal so treacherously?

Why Do the Wicked Prosper?

Have you noticed how many intriguing "why" questions we have? I suppose inquiring minds want to know why you need a driver's license to buy liquor when you shouldn't drink and drive. Or why isn't *phonetic* spelled the way it sounds? Why are there interstate highways in Hawaii? Why are there flotation devices under airplane seats instead of parachutes? You get the idea.

For Christians, there is a very common "why" question. Why do the wicked prosper? This is the question that plagued the prophet Jeremiah. As he looked at society, he saw the kings of Israel, the false shepherds who were misleading the people, living in palaces and eating the finest foods. He saw the prophets and priests, who were supporting the people in their sins instead of confronting them, employed in comfortable jobs and surrounded by an admiring populace. Why were those who lived contrary to God's will allowed to be happy and content?

Maybe you've asked the same question. It seems that the drug dealers and flesh peddlers have no financial problems. Why does God allow this? Those who defile the marriage bed and have no respect for their wedding vows seem to live happily. Why is that? Of course, the answer is the same today as it was in Jeremiah's day: judgment is coming (Jer. 12: 14). While these things are permitted for a season to test the faith of the righteous (v. 3), those who choose to ignore God's standards and flaunt their wicked lifestyle will someday have to face His wrath.

Be patient. Let these circumstances grow your trust in the Lord. Be confident that, at the right time, God will set the records straight. Those who live unrighteously will be judged and punished; those who live righteously will be vindicated and rewarded.

God uses the wicked to strengthen the resolve of the righteous.

Reflections/Prayer Requests

_____

_____

_____

_____

DAY 11

Jeremiah 13:23

Can the Ethiopian change his skin or the leopard its spots? Then may you also do good who are accustomed to do evil.

A Change of Nature

There's a legend about a scorpion, being a very poor swimmer, who asked a turtle to carry him on its back across the river. "Are you crazy?" exclaimed the turtle. "You'll sting me and I'll drown." "My dear turtle," laughed the scorpion, "if you were to drown, I'd go down with you. Now where's the logic in that?" "You're right," replied the turtle. "Hop on." The scorpion climbed aboard and halfway across the river gave the turtle a mighty sting. As they both sank to the bottom, the turtle inquired, "Do you mind if I ask you something? You said there is no logic in your stinging me. Why did you do it?" "It has nothing to do with logic," the drowning scorpion replied. "It's just my nature."

God realized this problem with the sin nature also applied to His people. Just as an Ethiopian couldn't change the dark color of his skin or a leopard remove the spots from its pelt, neither could God's people truly do good by themselves. On the surface they could make their actions appear good, but the problem lay deeper.

Just as skin color and fur markings are more than superficial adornments, the behavior of the Israelites reflected their sin nature. Their actions came out of a nature that was in rebellion against God.

Many unbelievers today are just like that. They do what appear to be kind and gracious acts. They give generously of their finances and time. But underneath it all is still a rebellious attitude toward God that taints all their actions. Only when our nature is changed are we capable of truly doing something good, and that takes a saving relationship with Christ.

Make sure that your relationship with the Lord is right, based on faith in Jesus Christ as Savior. Changing your outward behavior without your inward nature being transformed is just a cover-up. The substance is still the same. Only Jesus can make the inner man capable of doing what is truly good.

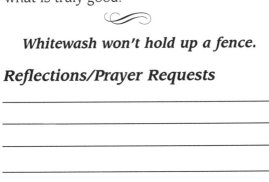

Whitewash won't hold up a fence.

Reflections/Prayer Requests

_____

_____

_____

_____

_____

_____

DAY 12

Jeremiah 14:14

And the LORD said to me, "The prophets prophesy lies in My name. I have not sent them, commanded them, nor spoken to them; they prophesy to you a false vision, divination, a worthless thing, and the deceit of their heart."

Whom Can You Believe?

In 1977 millions of people lined up at museums in various cities across the United States to view the treasures of the tomb of King Tutankhamen of Egypt. Later, Ali Hassan, curator of the Egyptian Museum in Cairo, discovered some of the jewels found in the tomb were not genuine. They were nothing but glass! When someone asked how this fact could go undetected for so many years, Mr. Hassan replied, "We were blinded by the gold. One just assumes that real gold and real gems go hand-in-hand. This is a case where they don't."

One would also assume that when a prophet claimed to speak for God he was telling the truth. But there are situations where that isn't the case either. Certain prophets may bear the title and dress the part, but they are fakes. God declared that many of the prophets in Jeremiah's time were speaking on their own. While they claimed to speak for the Lord, it was not true. They were speaking on their own initiative and weaving tales to deceive the people.

Jeremiah's day was not the only time when false prophets abounded. There are still many around today. Whether they go by the name of Jim Jones, David Koresh or Marshall Applewhite, they all have the same intent. Through clever deceptions they trick people into believing lies.

You need to be careful who and what you believe. Every teacher you hear, every person who speaks, every claim that is made, must be consistent with the truths of God's Word. If they aren't, they are the product of a false prophet.

Make sure that you test the spirits (1 John 4:1). Don't believe something because it appears true; believe it because God's Word says it is true.

Believe the Bible or you'll believe anything.

Reflections/Prayer Requests

_____

_____

_____

_____

_____

_____

DAY 13

Jeremiah 15:16

*Your words were found, and I ate them,
and Your word was to me the joy
and rejoicing of my heart; for I am called
by Your name, O LORD God of hosts.*

Called by His Name

It is a tremendous responsibility to bear someone's name. From the pages of history we learn of a cowardly young soldier in the army of Alexander the Great. Whenever the battle grew fierce, the young soldier would withdraw to safety. The general called him to account and asked, "What's your name, soldier?" When the timid soldier replied, "Alexander, sir," Alexander the Great sternly warned him, "Either change your name or change your ways."

Jeremiah proudly declared, "I am called by Your name, O LORD God of hosts." By this he meant, "I bear your name." Jeremiah's life reflected how seriously he took that privilege. In spite of opposition and, at times, physical persecution, he stood firm for God. The realization that he belonged to God was a constant reminder to Jeremiah that he needed to reflect His character. Unflinchingly he served his name's sake, even though, according to tradition, it ultimately resulted in him being placed in a hollow log and sawed in half.

Every Christian needs to remember that he or she bears the name of Christ. God's Word will be a joy to us when we seek to live in a way that does not bring shame to the name of our Lord. As we study His Word and make it a part of our daily lives, we will find our heart rejoicing in our relationship with Him. We will find it ever more precious that we are called by His name.

Never forget the name you bear—you are a "Christ"ian. If you want to find joy in that relationship, take time regularly to read God's Word. Prayerfully consider how you might live out that Word so you will show those around you what it means to be called by His name.

Every Christian bears Christ's name; live as an honor to His name.

Reflections/Prayer Requests

_____

_____

_____

_____

_____

_____

_____

DAY 14

Jeremiah 16:16-17

*"Behold, I will send for many fishermen,"
says the LORD, "and they shall fish them;
and afterward I will send for many hunters,
and they shall hunt them from every mountain
and every hill, and out of the holes of the
rocks. For My eyes are on all their ways;
they are not hidden from My face, nor is
their iniquity hidden from My eyes."*

Nothing Hidden

A man went to steal some corn from his neighbor's field. As a safeguard, he took his little boy with him to keep a lookout. Before beginning the heist, the man looked all around. Not seeing anyone, he ___ about to fill his bag when his son ___ ut, "Daddy, there's one way you ___ t looked yet!" The father, supposing ___ omeone was coming, asked his son ___ h way he meant. The young lad an- ___ red, "You haven't looked up!" Con- ___ ence-stricken, the father took his boy ___ the hand and hurried home without the ___ orn he had planned to take.

The people of Jeremiah's day were equally sure that they could commit their evil deeds without anyone knowing. But God warned them through His prophet that none of their iniquities were hidden from Him. Whichever way they might turn, whatever wickedness they might perpetrate, God's eye was on them. Even if they sought to hide under the waters, on the mountains or in a hole in the ground, God knew where to find them. Escape from His watchful gaze was impossible.

Technology today has increased astoundingly. Plastic surgeons can alter a person's appearance, and counterfeiters can provide fake identification. But God can't be eluded. His watchful eye can see through any disguise. The one who has deceived those around him has yet to reckon with the One above him. Others may be baffled, but God knows and sees it all.

If you feel a victim of deception, rest assured that God has not been taken in. He has seen every deceitful deed and will eventually bring the guilty party to account. No hiding place is so secure that God's eye cannot see; no guilty party so clever that God will not bring him to justice.

Only a fool thinks he can fool God.

Reflections/Prayer Requests

_____

_____

_____

_____

DAY 15

Jeremiah 17:9-10

"The heart is deceitful above all things, and desperately wicked; who can know it? I, the LORD, search the heart, I test the mind, even to give every man according to his ways, according to the fruit of his doings."

The Deceitful Heart

One summer the State of Delaware experimented with the honor system for 20 days on its turnpike. Motorists without exact change at the automatic tollbooths were allowed to take return envelopes and mail the money later. The Associated Press reported that in 20 days, more than 26,000 envelopes were taken but only 582 were returned. Of those returned, some had stamps or just pieces of paper instead of money. The experiment cost the state about $4,000 before it was discontinued, and that didn't include the lost tolls.

Israel also demonstrated a dishonest heart. With their lips the people claimed to worship God, but all their actions indicated otherwise. God accused them of building altars and erecting wooden idols under every green tree (Jer. 17:2). Jeremiah called their hearts "deceitful" and "desperately wicked." The word *deceitful* means "crooked, polluted or slippery." They simply couldn't be trusted. But even more tragic, this situation was terminal. The word translated "desperately wicked" is used elsewhere to mean "incurable" (2 Sam. 12:15; Jer. 15:18). They had untrustworthy hearts, and that would lead to their deaths.

The one thing that hasn't changed over the centuries is man's heart. If anything, it's gotten worse. Children are killing children. Racial groups try to eradicate one another in the name of ethnic cleansing. Cases of rape, abuse, sexually transmitted diseases and brutal crimes are on the rise. But there's hope. God knows our heart and He can make it pure.

Ask God to reveal to you anything in your heart that needs cleansing. Then apply the only substance that can wash your heart clean—the blood of Jesus.

The heart of the problem is the problem with the heart.

Reflections/Prayer Requests

_____

_____

_____

_____

_____

_____

DAY 16

Jeremiah 18:1-4

The word which came to Jeremiah from the LORD, saying: "Arise and go down to the potter's house, and there I will cause you to hear My words." Then I went down to the potter's house, and there he was, making something at the wheel. And the vessel that he made of clay was marred in the hand of the potter; so he made it again into another vessel, as it seemed good to the potter to make.

God of the Second Chance

Not long before she died in 1988, in a moment of surprising candor on television, Marghanita Laski, a well-known secular humanist and novelist, said, "What I envy most about you Christians is your forgiveness; I have nobody to forgive me."

Jeremiah pointed God's people toward this forgiveness as he shared his experience at the potter's house. While watching the craftsman at his work, he noticed that the vessel became marred. Yet the potter didn't throw away the clay. Instead, he took the flawed material and formed a different container. The same was true for Israel. God's original intent for His people was severely marred by their sin, yet He still had plans for them. When forgiven, they could still serve Him, but in a different way.

Sin always causes havoc in people's lives, including Christians. Sometimes the damage is so extensive that God cannot use those individuals as He originally desired, but He doesn't discard them. When they turn to Him for forgiveness, He can take those misshapen lumps and mold them into vessels for His use—different, perhaps, from what would have been His perfect will, yet useful nevertheless. God is the God of a second chance.

If you are in this condition, marred from the sin that's been in your life, don't despair. Look to God for forgiveness and a second chance. He can remold your life so you can still serve Him as a vessel of His choosing.

The God who made us also can remake us.

Reflections/Prayer Requests

_____

_____

_____

_____

_____

_____

_____

DAY 17

Jeremiah 20:9

*Then I said, "I will not make mention
of Him, nor speak anymore in His name."
But His word was in my heart like a burning
fire shut up in my bones; I was weary
of holding it back, and I could not.*

Fire in the Bones

For more than 20 years a fire has been burning deep within the earth of Centralia, a small community of 1,200 residents in the heart of Pennsylvania's anthracite coal fields. Fifteen federal, state and local agencies have spent more than $3.5 million to extinguish the flames without success. You can touch the earth and feel the heat. I have driven through the town to see smoke rising from the ground. Government officials have stopped trying to put out the fire; it's a futile task.

It was a fire like this that smoldered in the depths of Jeremiah's soul. After being accused and abused, God's servant decided simply to ignore the need around him. If people didn't want to hear what God had to say, he would oblige them. But it wasn't that simple. As he shut up God's words within him, they felt like a fire burning in his bones. Nothing was able to extinguish the flames. He had to express what God put in his heart.

This should be true for every Christian too. We should have a burning message in our hearts. Like an underground fire, God's message of salvation should be burning a hole in our souls. It is not a message the world will like to hear, and there may even be unpleasant consequences if we share it. But when a fire burns deep within you with no hope of quenching it, you simply must share the message. People need the Lord.

Pray that God will fan the flames in your soul today. Look for every opportunity to share the message in your heart, and when you find those opportunities, take them. Touch people's lives with your fire and spread the flames.

It's better to be ablaze for Jesus than smolder in quietness.

Reflections/Prayer Requests

_____

_____

_____

_____

_____

_____

_____

_____

_____

DAY 18

Jeremiah 21:8

"Now you shall say to this people, 'Thus says the LORD: "Behold, I set before you the way of life and the way of death."'"

The Choice

According to Aesop's fables, a long time ago when the world was young, the birds and the beasts were engaged in a bitter war. The bat, not wanting to be on the losing side—whichever that might turn out to be—tried to be on both sides. Whenever the birds won a battle, he would fly with them, telling everyone he was a bird. When the beasts won, he would walk around, assuring everyone that he was a beast. Because he refused to make a choice, he was rejected by both the birds and the beasts. From that day on, according to Aesop, the bat has had to go into hiding, living in dark caves, only daring to come out at night.

God instructed Jeremiah to put before the Israelites a choice. The armies of Nebuchadnezzar surrounded the city of Jerusalem. Those who defected to the Chaldeans, God said, would be spared; those who stayed in the city were doomed. This was the very opposite of what the people expected. Surely God would not allow His holy city to be conquered. They were faced with the choice of believing God as He spoke through Jeremiah or their false prophets, who assured them Jerusalem would not fall. One way was life, the other way was death, and there was no middle ground.

There are still many false prophets in the world. They speak eloquently of what God has done or will do. But their words don't square with God's words as found in the Bible. To choose the former is to choose death; to choose the latter is to choose life—but a choice must be made. Taking both sides is not an option.

Have you decided yet what you will choose? Make your choice today. Will it be the wisdom of the world, which brings the way of death? Or will it be the wisdom of God's Word, which brings the way of life? The choice is yours, but a choice must be made. You can't have it both ways.

When it comes to life and death, there's no third option.

Reflections/Prayer Requests

_____

_____

_____

_____

_____

DAY 19

Jeremiah 23:29

"Is not My word like a fire?" says the LORD, "and like a hammer that breaks the rock in pieces?"

A Hammer on a Rock

Hammers come in all shapes and sizes. There are jackhammers, sledgehammers, claw hammers and ball peen hammers, to name a few. Each one is designed with a certain task in mind. A jackhammer breaks up asphalt. A sledgehammer drives stakes into the ground. A claw hammer drives nails through lumber. A ball peen hammer is frequently used by machinists. But all hammers have one ultimate purpose: to enable the user to penetrate a hard substance.

As God viewed Israel in the time of Jeremiah, He saw a nation whose heart had become exceedingly hard. The kings (or shepherds) failed in their responsibility to lead the people as they ought. Instead of guiding them to green pastures, many of the kings led the people into the wilderness of idolatry and immorality (Jer. 23:1-2). Even the religious leaders, whose job was to exhort the people to righteousness, hardened their hearts against God. He declared that both prophet and priest were profane (v. 11). Something was needed to penetrate these callused hearts. That's why God proclaimed that His Word would not only be like a fire to burn away the chaff, but also like a hammer, powerful enough to shatter the rock-hard hearts of His people.

The Bible tells us that sin hardens the heart (Eph. 4:17-19). The longer a person rebels against God, the harder his heart becomes. But we must never underestimate the power of God's Word. Sometimes it touches our lives gently and brings comfort and healing. At other times it comes down like a sledgehammer with a blow that breaks our hearts into pieces. The more we choose to harden our hearts against God and His will, the more devastating the blow.

Ask God to reveal if your heart has become hardened toward Him. And if you sense it has, allow Him to use His Word to shatter any hardness you might find.

Better a shattered heart than a hardened heart.

Reflections/Prayer Requests

_____

_____

_____

_____

_____

DAY 20

Jeremiah 24:7

"Then I will give them a heart to know Me, that I am the LORD; and they shall be My people, and I will be their God, for they shall return to Me with their whole heart."

A Heart to Know God

A few years ago Kelly Perkins could hardly walk around the block, let alone climb a mountain. In 1995, however, she was the recipient of a heart transplant. Two years later she became the first heart-transplant patient to climb Mount Whitney, the highest mountain in the 48 contiguous states. Thanks to a new heart, the 36-year-old real estate appraiser was able to reach the top and return within three days. All this was done without any ill effects. What the old heart could never have accomplished, the new one did easily.

God promised that His people would someday receive a new heart as well. In place of their old, sin-clogged spiritual cardiovascular system, they would receive a new heart that would enable them to love the Lord and follow Him. This could not be accomplished by "reworking" the heart they already had, however. Israel needed a heart transplant and only God could do it.

This promise was fulfilled in the Lord Jesus Christ. When we receive Christ as our Savior, whether we are a Jew or a Gentile, God doesn't simply patch up the weak spots or plaster over the cracks. He doesn't simply remodel our old lives. He gives us new lives. He makes us into completely new creatures in Christ (2 Cor. 5:17). And that includes a new spiritual heart. What the old heart couldn't do, the new heart is able to accomplish with joy. Through the work of God's Spirit in your new heart, you can know and obey the Lord Jesus in a way that never could have been achieved with the old.

Give thanks to God for your new heart. Rejoice that now you can not only seek the Lord with all your heart, but you can obey Him with all your heart as well.

Only God can perform a spiritual heart transplant.

Reflections/Prayer Requests

_____

_____

_____

_____

_____

_____

_____

DAY 21

Jeremiah 29:13

And you will seek Me and find Me, when you search for Me with all your heart.

Seek and Find

A 911 operator received a call one evening but heard nothing on the line. Fearing the worst, she called back. A little boy answered the phone in a barely audibly voice. She said, "Hello. Did you just call 911?" The boy replied in a hushed tone, "No!" "Okay, is your mommy home?" "Yes," the boy whispered, "but she's busy talking to the police." "Oh, so the police are there? May I speak to one of them?" the operator asked. "No, they're all busy." "All right," she responded, "then is your daddy home?" "Yes, but he's busy talking to the firemen." "Well, could I speak to one of the firemen then, please?" "No," the lad said softly, "they're really busy too." "Goodness," the operator said, "what are all these people busy doing?" "Looking for me," the boy whispered back.

Jeremiah assured the people that God was not playing this kind of hide-and-seek with them. A day was coming, the prophet said, in which those who sincerely seek God would find Him. No longer would they have to go through intermediaries like Levitical priests or perform repetitive rituals. God would make Himself personally and directly available.

This happened when Christ died on Calvary's cross. The heavy veil that separated the Holy of Holies from the rest of the temple was split in two. The Holy of Holies was the most sacred part of the temple. It was here that the Ark of the Covenant, the symbol of God's presence, was kept. Yet this place, where previously only the high priest could enter, became open to anyone's view. The barrier between God and man was removed.

Take advantage of your opportunity to come directly into God's presence. He wants to have fellowship with you personally. Approach God with a sincere heart and hands washed clean from sin. You will find Him delighted to have your company.

When we hide ourselves in Christ, God never hides Himself from us.

Reflections/Prayer Requests

_____

_____

_____

_____

_____

_____

DAY 22

Jeremiah 30:7

Alas! For that day is great, so that none is like it; and it is the time of Jacob's trouble, but he shall be saved out of it.

Jacob's Trouble

Society is filled with offers for deliverance. If you have a toothache, a dentist can take care of it. If you have money problems, you can get help from a financial planner. If you have a headache, most stores carry a variety of medications designed to your relieve pain. But some troubles are so great that only God can bring deliverance.

It was this latter kind of deliverance that Jeremiah foresaw in the future for Israel. The Jewish people would go through many trials. In Jeremiah's day, the temple would be destroyed and the people would be taken to Babylon for a 70-year exile. Shortly after the time of Christ, Jerusalem was destroyed again (A.D. 70) and the Jews were scattered to the four corners of the earth. In the 20th century, these much-maligned people were decimated by the Nazi Holocaust. Jeremiah warned that a future time of trouble would distress Jacob, a symbol for Israel, much worse than anything they had experienced thus far. Yet the prophet concluded this fearsome prediction with a promise: "But he shall be saved out of it."

This is the promise that every believer can hold to as well. Even though the "time of Jacob's trouble" specifically refers to Israel, we all face our own troubles. And sometimes these difficulties become more severe than we can handle. Perhaps cancer strikes, or a loved one dies, or we lose our job and can't find another. In the midst of these tribulations, God assures us we shall be saved out of them.

If you are going through a trial that seems more severe than what you've ever faced before, look to God for deliverance. Take confidence in the promise that, at the right time, God will save you out of it. That's His word to you.

Keep looking up. Your redemption is drawing near.

Reflections/Prayer Requests

_____

_____

_____

_____

_____

_____

_____

_____

DAY 23

Jeremiah 31:3

The LORD has appeared of old to me, saying: "Yes, I have loved you with an everlasting love; therefore with lovingkindness I have drawn you."

An Everlasting Love

In his book *Make Your Life Worthwhile*, Richard Armstrong shares the story of a man in Wales who sought to win the affection of a certain woman for 42 years before she finally said yes. Year after year the persistent but rather shy man slipped a weekly love letter under his neighbor's door. But she continually refused to speak and mend the spat that had parted them decades before. After writing 2,184 love letters without ever getting a spoken or written answer, the single-hearted old man eventually summoned up enough courage to present himself in person. He knocked on the door of the reluctant lady and asked for her hand. To his delight and surprise, she accepted.

One has to wonder at God's attitude toward Israel. Over the centuries, He has pursued this obstinate group of people with very little encouragement. Certainly there have been individuals like Abraham, Moses and David who walked with Him, but for the most part His efforts have been rebuffed. Hardly would one generation wake up to their need for the Lord before the next would thumb their noses at Him again. Why would God persist in this lopsided relationship? Jeremiah says it's because of God's everlasting love.

Even today, Christians often fall far short of the righteousness that ought to characterize our lives. We become entangled with the things of the world; we fall into immorality; we bicker and fight among ourselves. Yet when we repent and seek God, He always receives us back. Why? Because He loves us with an everlasting love.

If you feel you've failed God once too often, if you're ready to toss in the towel, remember God's everlasting love. It's not a love just for the days you do everything right. It's not a love only for those people who have it all together. It's an everlasting love—and it's for you.

Never give up on God because He never gives up on you.

Reflections/Prayer Requests

_____

_____

_____

_____

_____

_____

DAY 24

Jeremiah 31:34

"No more shall every man teach his neighbor, and every man his brother, saying, 'Know the LORD,' for they all shall know Me, from the least of them to the greatest of them," says the LORD. "For I will forgive their iniquity, and their sin I will remember no more."

Blessed Amnesia

In February 1978, Steven Kubacki was cross-country skiing on the ice of Lake Michigan. He stopped for a moment, pausing to enjoy the winter solitude. As he stood there, he realized it was colder than he thought. Turning around, he started back, but came to realize he was lost. Wandering on the ice, he grew numb and very tired. The next thing he remembered was waking up in a field warmed by the touch of the springtime sun. The clothing he wore, the items in the backpack beside him, were all unfamiliar. It was 14 months later and he had no recollection of what had transpired during the intervening time. He lost more than a year of his life to total amnesia.

Jeremiah promised that God would one day have this same forgetfulness toward Israel's sin. While they would have to experience the consequences of their sin, the prophet indicated that something in the future would remove the guilt of sin forever. A day was coming when sin would be remembered no more.

When Christ died on the cross, this promise became a reality. With His last breath, Jesus proclaimed, "It is finished" (John 19:30). In the New Testament era, merchants would use these same words to indicate that a bill had been paid. The Father is able to put behind Him forever our sins because Jesus, His Son, paid the penalty for those sins. The Father was released to forget because Jesus paid the price.

If you are struggling with guilt over your sins, confess them and put them under the blood of Christ. Ask God to forgive you and, having done that, do what the Father does—forget them. Move on with your life and leave your sins in the past.

God forgets your confessed sins; so should you.

Reflections/Prayer Requests

_____

_____

_____

_____

_____

DAY 25

Jeremiah 32:27

*"Behold, I am the LORD, the God of all flesh.
Is there anything too hard for Me?"*

Nothing Too Hard

A rather sickly woman had been deserted by her husband. He left her with three preschool children, a mangy dog, a broken-down, second-floor flat and many bills. One morning she discovered that the mutt had chosen her only good pair of shoes as a chew stick. The youngest baby had cried the night through with colic. As she was preparing breakfast, the power went off because the bill hadn't been paid. Then the dog decided to play tug of war with the tablecloth, pulling all the dishes and food onto the floor. Just then she heard a commotion out in the street. Running to the kitchen, she opened the window and a man below yelled out, "Garbage man." Her only reply was, "Okay, send it up."

Times were like that for Jerusalem too. The Chaldeans had raised siege mounds around the city. Famine and pestilence stalked the streets. Jeremiah was on the verge of losing all hope for survival. His whole life seemed like a garbage heap—and each day only added a little more to the pile. But in the midst of this doom and gloom, God said to him, "Is there anything too hard for Me?" Even preserving the prophet's life in the midst of disaster was not an impossible task for God.

Life gets rough sometimes. Illness strikes, financial troubles threaten us, family problems dog our steps. At best, most people just hope they can scramble to the top as each new load of garbage gets dumped on them. But you don't have to live like that. God says, "Things can be better for you because I am with you—and nothing is too difficult for Me." Even your most troublesome circumstances simply become a stage on which God demonstrates that nothing is hopeless with Him.

If your situation is causing you to despair, listen to what the Lord has to say to you: "Is anything too hard for Me?" Take confidence in the fact that the omnipotent God is on your side.

When God says "nothing is too hard," He means "nothing"!

Reflections/Prayer Requests

_____

_____

_____

_____

_____

_____

DAY 26

Jeremiah 33:3

*"Call to Me, and I will answer you,
and show you great and mighty things,
which you do not know."*

Simply Call

Years ago there was a great drought in Connecticut. The water disappeared from the hills, and the farmers drove their cattle into the valleys. Streams there began to fail, and the neighbors said to a certain godly man, "You must not send your flocks down here anymore." The old man gathered his family around the kitchen table and, kneeling by their chairs, they cried with tears and supplications for water that the flocks and herds might not perish. Afterward he went out into the hills, and in a place where he had walked many times before, he saw that the ground was dark and moist. When he dug up the soil, water started to bubble to the surface. The family came with pails and watered the stock; then they made troughs reaching to the house. Water was plentiful. God's people called, and He answered.

The prophet Jeremiah was also in distressing circumstances. He was in a city under siege. To make matters worse, he had been put in prison because of his counsel to surrender to the Chaldeans. Everywhere he turned there was danger and opposition. But God assured him, "Call to Me and I will answer." And God did. He delivered the prophet both from prison and from the hands of his enemies.

Far too many Christians fail to take God up on His promise. Prayerlessness is a common problem in the church today. God, however, will not do His part until we do ours. We do not call; therefore, God does not answer (James 4:2). As a result, we do not see the wonderful things God wants to show us.

Commit yourself to call on God in prayer. Be consistent. Be courageous. Be confident. Then when you pray, God will show you "great and mighty things."

There cannot be an answer until there is a prayer.

Reflections/Prayer Requests

_____

_____

_____

_____

_____

_____

_____

_____

DAY 27

Jeremiah 36:4

Then Jeremiah called Baruch the son of Neri-ah; and Baruch wrote on a scroll of a book, at the instruction of Jeremiah, all the words of the LORD which He had spoken to him.

The Inspired Word of God

A first-grade girl was sitting next to her grandmother during the morning worship service. Curious, she looked down at her grandmother's open Bible. In a low whisper, she asked, "Did God really write that?" "Yes," her grandmother whispered back. Looking down at the pages of the Bible again, the little girl said in amazement, "Wow! He really has neat handwriting!"

That's obviously not what we mean when we say that the Bible was written by God. Instead, Jeremiah more accurately demonstrates the process of inspiration. The words written down were spoken by Jeremiah, but they didn't originate with him. Everything that the prophet instruct-ed the scribe Baruch to write were words that the Lord had given to Jeremiah. God chose the content; Jeremiah was simply the instrument by which that message was recorded.

When you open God's Word, remember that what you read is not the opinions or thoughts of those who penned them. Second Timothy 3:16 says that all Scripture is given by "inspiration of God." Literally, this phrase means "God-breathed." Nothing comes more deeply from within us than our breath. Therefore, the Bible has as its source the innermost depths of God Himself. While the Scriptures pass through the intellect and personality of the writer, they have their origin in God. If you disagree with the Bible, you're not disagreeing with the likes of David and Paul and Jeremiah. You're disagreeing with God.

As you read your Bible, never forget how special that book you hold really is. The Bible is God's personal, intimate Word to you. When you read it, you are touched by the breath of God.

The Word of God is the breath of God.

Reflections/Prayer Requests

_____

_____

_____

_____

_____

_____

_____

_____

DAY 28

Jeremiah 37:16-17

When Jeremiah entered the dungeon and the cells, and Jeremiah had remained there many days, then Zedekiah the king sent and took him out. The king asked him secretly in his house, and said, "Is there any word from the LORD?" And Jeremiah said, "There is." Then he said, "You shall be delivered into the hand of the king of Babylon!"

A Word From the Lord

Someone once said the trouble with most of us is that we would rather be ruined by praise than saved by criticism. It is far more comfortable to hear what we want to hear than to be told what we sometimes need to hear.

Jeremiah was faced with this dilemma when called before King Zedekiah. The prophet already had been beaten and placed for many days in a dungeon for speaking the truth (Jer. 37:11-15). No one could blame him if he weren't eager to return there. So when the king wanted to know if the Lord had given any word, it must have been very tempting for Jeremiah to say only what he knew Zedekiah wanted to hear. But faithful preachers and prophets can't do that. Jeremiah spoke the truth instead. He wasn't willing to sugarcoat God's Word in order to make his life temporarily more comfortable.

God never promised we would always make friends or be popular when we share His Word. In fact, often the opposite occurs. The world would much rather have their beliefs confirmed than challenged. It should come as no surprise, then, that people sometimes respond very negatively. Unfortunately, too often God's servants choose to avoid the truth or make it more palatable to the world. Either leads to tragedy.

Commit yourself to speaking the truth, even if it means going against popular opinion. Be willing to say what the world needs to hear, even when it doesn't want to hear it.

Truth can't be judged on the basis of popularity.

Reflections/Prayer Requests

_____

_____

_____

_____

_____

_____

_____

_____

DAY 29

Jeremiah 44:16-17

*"As for the word that you have spoken to us in the name of the L*ORD*, we will not listen to you! But we will certainly do whatever has gone out of our own mouth, to burn incense to the queen of heaven and pour out drink offerings to her, as we have done, we and our fathers, our kings and our princes, in the cities of Judah and in the streets of Jerusalem. For then we had plenty of food, were well-off, and saw no trouble."*

The Queen of Heaven

A young Christian girl who had worked for years in the fast-food business had a tendency toward absent-mindedness. One Sunday evening at a youth fellowship, the pastor called on her to bless the evening snacks. The room became quiet, heads were bowed and eyes closed. The girl began her prayer with, "Welcome to Mc-Donalds. May I take your order?"

While this is humorous, this girl may have reflected a more popular attitude toward God than she realized.

Even though Jeremiah's generation knew nothing about fast-food chains, they still exhibited the same mentality. The god whom they wanted to worship was the one who served the best hamburger in the shortest amount of time. In their eyes, the

God who Jeremiah represented wasn't a very good restaurateur. His service couldn't compete with the queen of heaven. She served plenty of food, prosperity and peace; He brought trials, tribulation and trouble. It was obvious where they would choose to eat.

We Christians need to search our own hearts. Do we worship God because He serves us the things we like? If the food were to go bad and the service become lousy, would we still be willing to sit at His table? What would happen if it were no longer the most popular place in town?

Commit your heart to seek the Lord not for what you can get, but for who He is. When it comes to your spiritual food, God is more interested in serving steak than flipping hamburger.

Don't settle for fast food when you can feast at God's banquet.

Reflections/Prayer Requests

DAY 30

Jeremiah 45:5

"And do you seek great things for yourself? Do not seek them; for behold, I will bring adversity on all flesh," says the LORD. "But I will give your life to you as a prize in all places, wherever you go."

Seeking Great Things

Former Miami Dolphins coach Don Shula took his wife on vacation to a small seaside town in Maine. Shula thought that surely far from Miami they could relax anonymously. It was raining when they arrived, so they decided to take in a movie. As they entered the small theater, the show had not yet started and the lights were still up. To their surprise, the scattered handful of people applauded their entrance. After they were seated Don said to his wife with as much humility as he could muster, "I guess there's nowhere I'm not known." A man seated nearby reached over and shook Don's hand. Shula said, "I have to admit I'm surprised that you know me here." The man replied, "Should I know you? We're just happy to see you folks because the manager said he wasn't going to start the movie until at least two more people showed up."

The emptiness of fame and fortune also was brought home to Baruch, the man who served as Jeremiah's scribe. As Jerusalem faced imminent destruction, God spoke through the prophet to remind the faithful secretary that every material thing would be lost. The power and positions of authority that had been sought for so eagerly would no longer exist. The Chaldeans would take all that away. Yet Baruch's life would be spared.

Christians can be sidetracked into seeking popularity and wealth as well. Yet God's Word says that ultimately all these things will be destroyed (2 Pet. 3:10). The only thing we can take out of this world will be the lives we have built on the Word of God.

Does Baruch's experience speak to you? Ask God to help you put your priorities in the right order. Rather than seeking those things that eventually will be destroyed, seek for a life that will bring eternal rewards.

If we don't live for what lasts, we'll live for far less.

Reflections/Prayer Requests

_____

_____

_____

_____

_____

DAY 31

Jeremiah 50:34

*Their Redeemer is strong; the LORD of hosts
is His name. He will thoroughly plead their
case, that He may give rest to the land,
and disquiet the inhabitants of Babylon.*

Our Strong Redeemer

Depending on how you choose to measure strength, it could be said that Chris Lawton of Solihull, England, is the strongest man in the world. According to the *1998 Guinness Book of Records*, Lawton bench-pressed 1,181,312 pounds over a 12-hour period.

Yet this record pales in significance when God is taken into account. Jeremiah declared that even though Israel was now oppressed, it wouldn't always be that way. The armies of Nebuchadnezzar were potent fighting machines, but they could do only what God allowed them to do. There would come a time when the sword would be turned against the Chaldeans and the inhabitants of Babylon (Jer. 50:35-37). The strong Redeemer of Israel, the Lord of hosts, would rise up and in the day of reckoning restore His people to their land. All the mighty armies in the world would not keep that from happening.

When disasters come crashing into our lives, we sometimes question God's power. We think, *If God is so strong, why did this happen?* Yet God assures us that whatever happens, He is strong enough to deal with it. Even though He allows powerful forces to discipline and chastise us, when the time is right, these same powers cannot stand against His judgments. While God may use the strength of others to work His will, none are stronger than He.

Do not judge God's strength by what you see. While the forces of evil may seem to be overwhelming, they are but instruments in God's omnipotent hands. When God permits difficulties to come into your life, it's not because He's not powerful enough to stop them. When that trial has done its work, God's power will take it away. Trust Him. No one is stronger than God.

With the power of God within us, we need never fear the powers around us.

Reflections/Prayer Requests

_____

_____

_____

_____

_____

_____

GIANTS OF THE OLD TESTAMENT